ANCIENT CORNWALL

A Guide to the **BEST** Sites

PETE LONDON

TOR MARK

Published by Tor Mark Ltd,
United Downs Industrial Estate,
St Day, Redruth, Cornwall TR16 5HY

www.tormark.co.uk

First published 2013,
Second edition 2022, reprinted 2024

ISBN 978 0 85025 465 5

Printed and bound in the UK

 FSC Printed on FSC Mix

CORNWALL'S ANCIENT STONES

The far-flung peninsula of Penwith forms Cornwall's western tip. By turn wild or sun-softened, the landscape varies from brooding greys to summer's heathland radiance, and unbelievably vivid skies. To the east, Bodmin Moor's crags and wide spaces breathe myth; hamlets and farmsteads huddle in shallow valleys, along narrow, twisting lanes. Both places are isolated and moody, but magnificent.

It's not just the scenery which captivates; the two areas are home to a mass of ancient riches, some of Britain's finest prehistoric stone sites. Other parts of Cornwall too have their share of monuments, thousands of years old. The great stones are a winner for walks and discovering, and inspire an emotional connection which may surprise you. This little book is a glimpse at the Duchy's most spectacular ancient sites, and the countryside which makes exploring such an unforgettable experience.

BELOW:
THE MÊN AN TOL, PENWITH'S MYSTERIOUS HOLED MONUMENT, PROBABLY APPEARED DURING BRONZE AGE TIMES AND TODAY IS A FAVOURITE CALL FOR WALKERS – BUT WHAT WAS IT FOR?

HOW OLD ARE THE STONES?

ABOVE:
BOSCAWEN-UN
CIRCLE

Cornwall's stones fall into three archaeological eras. During Neolithic times, say between four and six thousand years ago, our ancestors left their wandering hunter-gatherer existence and began to build permanent communities. Farms appeared, crops were grown on cleared areas, animals raised: goats, pigs, cattle. And as people settled down, they began to leave their mark on the landscape.

Cornwall's earliest sites are Neolithic: huge stone burial chambers or quoits, several of which survive today, and tor enclosures, hilltop havens guarded by vast defensive ramparts. Burial tombs too were first built in the Neolithic period though others appeared later.

The Bronze Age, between around 2,000 and 600 BC, saw the arrival of the new alloy made from copper and tin. Early bronze items were rare marks of social status but slowly the metal became more widespread, used for tools and weapons. Cornwall's beautiful stone circles were created during the Bronze Age, possibly even earlier, imposing granite rings forming places of worship, ceremony or ritual.

Great upright standing stones also appeared, often solitary sentinels but sometimes in pairs; were they memorials, territorial markers or maybe even forms of totem-pole? The first round house settlements too date from Bronze Age times, clusters of family dwellings with circular stone walls, covered by coned roofs of thatch.

Gradually, for tools and weapons bronze was replaced by a more durable, versatile metal: iron. The Iron Age dawned about the 7th century BC; by the mid 1st century BC Julius Caesar had landed at what is now Kent. For much of Britain the following time is known as the Roman period, but the occupiers influenced distant Cornwall so little that we can treat the Duchy's Iron Age as continuing until they withdrew to mainland Europe, around 400 AD. Over that era, across Cornwall complex defended settlements were constructed: hill forts built by local chieftains to dominate or protect their territory, and promontory forts adapted from coastal headlands.

From around 100 AD courtyard house settlements also developed in Cornwall, groups of thick stone-walled dwellings with separate storage rooms and byres for animals, all facing inwards onto open yards sometimes paved with massive slabs. These tiny villages were a form of community unique in mainland Britain.

BELOW:
ON THE RISE BETWEEN MÊN AN TOL AND DING DONG, BOSKEDNAN CIRCLE'S BRONZE AGE STONES POINT SKYWARD LIKE ANCIENT TEETH.

QUOITS: PREHISTORIC TOMBS

Sited mostly on Penwith's granite uplands are its mighty Neolithic quoits, great stone tombs with inner burial chambers built above ground, which may be up to 5,000 years old. Several are still with us; best-known is Lanyon (SW 430337) between Madron and Morvah villages, its huge capstone borne by three uprights. During a violent storm in 1815 Lanyon collapsed, but nine years later was re-erected by public subscription. Apparently a mounted horseman could pass beneath its original form so today's arrangement is slightly smaller, but the stone still holds great mystery, standing solitary in its remote field.

Most imposing of Penwith's quoits is lonely Zennor (SW 469380). Jagged and brutal, it's a mile or so's tramp from the village of the same name, up a harsh thorny rise to a stone plateau and flat mottled moorland. The massive monument sits implacable against all weathers; from nearby Zennor, Hill a patchwork of ancient stone-edged fields runs down to the cliff tops and blue Atlantic.

We're lucky Zennor's still reasonably intact; during the 1860s a local farmer began to dismantle it, intending to build a cattle shed using the stones. Fortunately the vicar of Zennor William Borlase, great-grandson of early local antiquary Dr Borlase of Ludgvan, intervened and for the bribe of five shillings (25p) the farmer went elsewhere for his materials.

LANYON QUOIT'S STARK
SIMPLICITY, SET AGAINST THE MOST
CORNISH OF SKIES.

Mulfra quoit (SW 451353) sits atop a rise north of Newmill village, three upright slabs with a great crooked capstone reaching toward the sky. But of Penwith's quoits Chûn (SW 402339) is least-spoiled, its mushroom profile squatting on a hilltop east of Woon Gumpus Common. Cornish legend tells us that long ago Chûn's capstone served as a dinner-table for the Duchy's fabled giants, as they crunched on whole sheep or goats. Today the spot's still good for a snack but you'll have to take your own picnic; the nearest shops are a couple of miles away, down at Pendeen village on the beautiful B3306 northern coast road.

Cornwall's quoits were once partly-covered by domes of soil or cairns, the edges of which were marked by flat kerb stones. It's thought the entrances to the quoits' internal chambers were left exposed, to put on view a part of their great stone structures.

RIGHT:
BODMIN'S GRAND TRETHEVY
QUOIT LOOMS AT YOU FROM ITS
PODIUM.

Today, around Chûn quoit you can still spot evidence of its kerbed boundary.

In mid-Cornwall, at Bodmin Moor's southern side near the hamlets of Crows Nest and Darite, you'll find Trethevy quoit (SX 259688).

The sloping capstone, all 11 tons of it, is supported by six huge side slabs; it's pierced by a small round hole which today is still a puzzle to us. Trethevy's inner chamber is enclosed and fronted by a small antechamber or portal, in the same way as Zennor. The quoit stands on the remains of a broad plinth, its raised elevation overbearing as you gaze upward; there are several theories, but just how did the old people transport such colossal stones?

BELOW:
MULFRA QUOIT FORMS THE END OF A
GLORIOUS WALK FROM THE MÊN AN TOL,
THOUGH YOU MAY LIKE TO WAIT FOR
WARMER WEATHER. ALTERNATIVELY, CLIMB
THE SLOPES NORTH OF NEWMILL VILLAGE
TO SEE IT.

CORNWALL'S LEAST DISTURBED QUOIT
IS CHÛN, WHICH PERCHES ON A
SUBSTANTIAL RISE. FROM THE WEST
IT'S EASILY PICKED OUT AGAINST THE
SKYLINE.

TOR ENCLOSURES:
FORTRESS SANCTUARIES

Cornwall's tor enclosures also appeared during Neolithic times, say between 4,000 and 3,000 BC. Several were built, hilltop tribal centres protected by massive banks of stone, and their ruins can still be seen. The largest are at Carn Brea near Redruth, Helman Tor between Bodmin and Lostwithiel, Stowe's Pound outside Minions, and Rough Tor (pronounce it Row, as in chart music) near Camelford.

Up on Carn Brea's rocky brow (SW 685408), the man-made ramparts aren't always easy to distinguish from surrounding natural outcrops. Summer bracken tends to hide the defensive remains, though you'll quickly spot Iron Age hut circles and small standing stones. But a trip to the top is also worthwhile to admire the Basset monument, the great granite needle visible from miles away, together with bijou Carn Brea Castle, today a restaurant; the enclosure connects the two points. Views are panoramic, taking in St Agnes Beacon, Redruth town and time-softened ruins from the days of tin and copper mining. Carn Brea and its historic surroundings now form a World Heritage site.

In mid-Cornwall south of the A30 Lanivet junction, wriggling lanes pass through Reperry Cross and Trebell Green to mighty Helman Tor (SX 062616). A footpath leads you up nearly 700 feet (213m) to the enclosure's remains but there's also a narrow track, with parking at the summit. On Helman's two-acre top the remnants of low ramparts survive, as well as roughly-levelled areas forming terraces, perhaps once bases for dwellings. Again undergrowth disguises the ruins, which are only partly man-made. Within their enclosures the old people often incorporated natural rock formations where they could – why make even more work?

Helman's huge stones are surreal, sculpted and split by the elements, their stacks spread across the hill. You'll see Padstow to the north and southwards to Fowey, as well as Dartmoor's plains far in the east. With luck too you'll meet sturdy ponies; as they graze, they like to shelter in the lee of the boulders. Today Helman forms part of the captivating Saints' Way recreational footpath between Padstow and Fowey. It's also the hub of Cornwall Wildlife Trust's Wilderness Trail nature reserve, a mosaic of habitats from wetlands to rolling heath and a real gem of the Duchy's natural world.

Just east of Camelford, lofty granite Rough Tor (SX 147808) is another good centre for exploring. The remains of its enclosure walls can be traced between the two rock-strewn peaks, Rough Tor itself and to the north-east, Little Rough Tor. These days, there's some doubt as to when the enclosure was created. Until recently considered Neolithic, currently some experts feel it could be early Bronze Age, perhaps part of the treasure of antiquities clustered round the hill's base.

Not far away, on Bodmin Moor's south-eastern side, Minions is Cornwall's highest village at around 1,000 feet (305m). There you'll find Stowe's Pound (SX 259725), two hilltop enclosures with stone ramparts hundreds of yard long, walls which once stood maybe 10 feet high (3m). Again, the remains date from Neolithic or possibly early Bronze Age times. The views are breath-taking, across Dartmoor to the Lizard peninsula far in the south-west.

Like Cornwall's other main tor enclosures, within its walls Stowe's Pound shows evidence of hut dwellings, areas cleared to allow building, and is set among huge wildly-eroded natural stones. At its southern end by a disused granite quarry you'll encounter Minions' famous Cheesewring, the topsy-turvy formation which looks as if it could topple over at any moment. Kids of all ages can have their photograph taken in its shadow, but be quick!

BELOW:
NEAR MINIONS, STOWE'S POUND ENCLOSURE IS DEFINED BY RAMPARTS BUILT FROM THOUSANDS OF STONES, BEHIND WHICH ARE GRASSY AREAS ONCE LEVELLED TO FORM LIVING-SPACE.

ENTRANCE GRAVES AND BURIAL BARROWS

In West Penwith around a dozen entrance graves survive; they stem from Neolithic times but were sometimes added to later. The sites differ, but often consisted of a sizeable mound of earth or stone, roughly circular or oval in plan, with a stone-lined entrance leading to the burial chamber. Inside, burial boxes or cists fashioned from granite slabs have sometimes been found.

One of the best-known Cornish entrance graves is Tregiffian (SW 430244) on the B3315 lane near Lamorna, its entrance surmounted by a heavy stone lintel, with a passage below toward the centre. Two similar monuments survive at Treen (SW 438371), south of Gurnard's Head, and at Pennance (SW 448376) near Zennor.

Burial barrows emerged during the Bronze Age. Our ancestors liked variety and built many types, including bowl, bell, curbed and ring barrows. Again the barrows' distinctive domes were constructed either from earth or stone; often they were elaborate inside, and like their Neolithic predecessors, some were developed in stages.

TOP RIGHT: **RILLATON BARROW, BETWEEN MINIONS AND STOWE'S POUND.**

BOTTOM RIGHT:
NEAR LAMORNA, TREGIFFIAN ENTRANCE GRAVE IS SITED BY THE ROADSIDE. BUT THIS IS A WEST PENWITH LANE SO DON'T BE PUT OFF; IT'S GENERALLY QUIET, ALWAYS SCENIC.

BY CAPE CORNWALL, ST JUST'S
BALLOWALL BARROW IS HUGE AND MAKES
A GREAT PICNIC SPOT. ON A GOOD DAY
YOU'LL SEE THE ISLES OF SCILLY.

Penwith's Ballowall barrow is near St Just (SW 355312). Ballowall may have started life as an entrance grave; a mammoth project, it was built from thousands of stones over many phases and probably ran way over its Bronze Age budget. The site was discovered in the 1870s under a waste-heap from nearby mining works. Investigated brutally by ham-fisted local antiquarian William Copeland Borlase and much altered, nonetheless Ballowall's is still impressive. The spot overlooks Cape Cornwall, Britain's only cape, with its incessant crashing waves and sauce-bottle mine-chimney; you'll also see the Land's End and Longships lighthouse.

On Bodmin Moor, the largest surviving round barrow is Bronze Age Rillaton (SX 260719), a short walk from Minions village. Some 35 yards (32m) across, the barrow's around 10 feet tall (3m) with a prominent stone-lined entrance and its top depressed after several visits from stone-robbers. Rillaton was excavated in 1837 though again clumsily by current standards; even so, several discoveries survived their ordeal including a bronze dagger, beads, pottery and glass items.

Also unearthed was the famous Rillaton Cup, fashioned of solid gold. The cup is similar to Bronze Age vessels found in the Aegean, suggesting Cornish contact with the ancient Eastern Mediterranean world. Via its temporary disappearance to the dressing-room of King George V, who 'borrowed' it to contain his collar-studs, Cornwall's priceless artefact is now kept by the British Museum; a replica is on show at the Royal Cornwall Museum in Truro.

Today, beneath its great lintel, Rillaton's aperture has just enough space to crawl through; it's simpler if you go in backwards. Down at Penwith, Tregiffian's grave is easy to enter while at Ballowall you can climb up over the high protective outer ring, and drop into the central interior chambers.

RIGHT:
RILLATON CUP, FOUND IN RILLATON BARROW,
IS SOLID GOLD AND ALMOST UNIQUE IN
BRITAIN.

STONE CIRCLES

Penwith is renowned for its enchanting stone circles, perhaps used by our ancestors for ceremony or rites; often they were built near barrows and standing stones. Easy to discover are the Merry Maidens (SW 432245) by the B3315 Newlyn to Treen lane, in legend said to be young women turned to granite for daring to dance on the Sabbath. They're still beautiful today, a perfect ring of nineteen Bronze Age boppers frozen in their field for all time; after rain, the grey stones gleam and glisten.

The Penwith circles' names are other-worldly, dreamlike, among them Boskednan by Carn Galva's summit; Boscawen-ûn – say it BoscaNOON – near St Buryan; and Tregeseal, below Carn Kenidjack's tormented outcrops. Whenever I can, armed with camera and sandwiches, I walk the narrow footpaths to visit them.

Boscawen-ûn (SW 412274) is serene, off-road down a gentle moorland incline, its stones radiant against lush surrounding greenery. Ovoid rather than truly circular and again with 19 perimeter stones, at its widest Boscawen-ûn is nearly 80 feet (24m) across. Under the great sloping centre stone you'll often see small votive offerings, generally wild flowers. Once I found a child's doll placed there, small and knitted with arms flung out, bleached by sun and showers, undisturbed.

Boskednan circle (SW 434351) sits by an arching footpath connecting Ding Dong's old tin mine with the enigmatic Mên an Tol site. Also known as the Nine Maidens and Penwith's highest ring, today Boskednan consists of eleven stones; sadly, over

time others have been snaffled by local stone splitters or miners. But the survivors are atmospheric, the walking beautiful; eastwards a shallow plain drops away toward Bodrifty's Iron Age settlement and Mulfra Quoit.

Near Truthwall village, Tregeseal circle (SW 386324) too is striking; it's been restored and the result is well-preserved. From Truthwall Hill a footpath takes you past Kenidjack's great rocks into a little gorse-filled dip, where once there were three rings. Near Tregeseal you'll find several burial mounds and the small mysterious Kenidjack holed stones (SW 390326).

To the east on Bodmin Moor, Stannon (SX 125800) and Fernacre (SX 145799) circles are still reasonably intact; both are within walking distance of Rough Tor's car park (SX 138819). Fernacre is large, with 35 stones upright from a total of 52. In the shadow of an old china-clay mining spoil heap, Stannon ring is even bigger with 81 stones, of which nearly half still stand. A couple of miles south, Leaze circle (SX 137773) is near the mystifying site known as King Arthur's Hall. And in the background much of the time is great Brown Willy, its name corrupted from the Cornish Bron Wennyly meaning Hill of Swallows, the Duchy's highest point at 1,377 feet (420m).

Off the A30 just east of the Bodmin turning, along a tiny bumpy lane are the Bronze Age Trippet Stones (SX 131750). The slabs form a true circle and of today's twelve survivors eight are upright. In the centre of the monument sits a small cuckoo, a recent granite boundary-marker. Pools sometimes encircle the standing stones, the ground worn away by wandering cows using them as rubbing-posts.

But Bodmin Moor's most spectacular circles are The Hurlers (SX 258714), just outside Minions. In fact there are three rings, running south-west to north-east. As you approach, the southernmost has only two stones still standing but the oval middle circle, with a greatest diameter of around 45 yards (41m), has 14 upright stones. The northern ring is over 35 yards (32m) across, with 11 uprights and 4 prone slabs. It's an amazing complex, the circles' horse-nibbled plain counterpointed by distant rearing hills.

In Cornish folklore, again the stones were once people but this time were men punished for playing a hurling match on the Sabbath. Local villagers loved the ball-throwing and carrying game which makes rugby look soft; despite the warnings of local holy man St Cleer, one Sunday they turned out for a fixture. Enraged by such sacrilege, St Cleer smote the ground with his staff and as an awful warning to others, instantly the players were turned to granite.

Away from the main stone sites near the port of Looe, you'll find a formation unique in shape and beauty: the Duloe circle (SX 236583), outside the village of the same name. Once known as The Druids' Circle it's Cornwall's smallest, the ovoid diameter at most around 12 yards (11m). But among the seven white quartz stones still standing are some of the Duchy's tallest, including one of over eight feet (2.5m) above ground; they're arranged as alternating large and small stones, all tapering toward the sky.

RIGHT:
BETWEEN THE LOOE AND WEST LOOE RIVERS
SITS DULOE CIRCLE. THE STONES' GUARDIAN
KEEPS A WATCHFUL EYE OUT.

STANDING STONES

Also dating from the Bronze Age are Cornwall's lofty standing stones, sometimes called longstones. As a rule they're solitary but occasionally come in pairs; usually they're much taller than the stones chosen for Cornwall's circles. What were they for? Experts disagree, though some were certainly grave-markers or memorials for prominent people. But the stones may have denoted territorial boundaries or acted as way-markers, while it has also been suggested their purpose was similar to Native American totem poles.

You'll find the biggest in Penwith, near Lamorna's Merry Maidens circle; in legend the two Pipers (SW 435248) were the dancing girls' backing duo, who came to a similar bad end. The larger is a giant at 15 feet (4.5m) tall while its partner, around 100 yards (91m) across the field, reaches 13½ feet (4m). The 11-foot (3.5m) Blind Fiddler near Sancreed (SW 425282) was also formerly a musician, another errant artiste who paid for striking up on the Sabbath. And along from the Mên an Tol, the standing stone known as Mên Scryfa (SW 427353) – Cornish for 'written stone' – may stem from Bronze Age times. Mên Scryfa bears a Latinised Cornish inscription which reads RIALOBRANI CVNOVALI FILI or 'The grave of Rigalobranos son of Cunoualos', probably a local chieftain.

On Bodmin Moor two tall stones stand at Minions, near the Hurlers circles; again, in folklore at times the pair are portrayed as ex-musicians – or were they members of the local hurling team, fleeing in vain before St Cleer's fury? And just west of the village you'll find the odd Minions longstone (SX 255706), sometimes called Long Tom.

It's nearly 10 feet (3m) tall and inscribed with a cross symbol, though it may have been erected during the Bronze Age.

Away from the main centres, several other standing stones survive. High on St Breock's moors near Wadebridge in mid-Cornwall, the Mên Gurta longstone (SW 968683), or in Cornish 'Stone of Waiting' is over 9 feet tall (2.7m) and the Duchy's heaviest ancient stone still upright, weighing in at a massive 17 tons. Mên Gurta sits among more than

90 barrows scattered across the downs, while a little to the east there's a smaller standing stone of just under 7 feet (2.1m).

On the Lizard, by Goonhilly's satellite station, is Dry Tree longstone (SW 726212). A real rarity in that part of the world, Dry Tree is around 10 feet tall (3m) and sits just outside the station's perimeter fence. It's positioned among burial mounds, at one of the moorland's highest points. Dry Tree is unusual in being fashioned from gabbro, a hard crystalline rock distinct from granite, the nearest source of which is two miles from its site; to move it must have been a literally monumental effort.

ON THE LIZARD, DRY TREE STANDING
STONE CAN BE FOUND BY GOONHILLY
SATELLITE STATION'S HIGH FENCE.

DEFENCES: HILL AND PROMONTORY FORTS

Cornwall's Bronze Age people, we may suppose, lived relatively peacefully. They settled and farmed, and found enough spare time to create their places of ritual or worship. But during the Iron Age a need grew for self-defence from other tribes or overseas raiders; fortifications were built by local chieftains to give refuge during outbreaks of trouble. The sites may also have been used as meeting-places, for trading, or ceremonially.

Explore along muddy paths shared with bird and animal travellers and you'll still find evidence of Cornwall's hill and promontory forts. One of the most intact is Chûn Castle (SW 405339), high on a windswept hilltop directly east from the quoit, its much older neighbour. A heavyweight circular stronghold over 85 yards (78m) in diameter, its inner defensive wall was once perhaps 10 feet (3m) or more tall. The castle is granite-built rather than the usual earthworks of its time, and may have helped defend Penwith's early tin workings. Its entrance is marked by huge paving slabs, and great posts which still stand.

In fact much survives at Chûn: outer and inner fortifications; remains of rooms, huts or houses; a stone-lined well which ensured water supply. The castle would have stayed in even better shape, but during the 1830s some of its stonework was purloined by the builders of nearby Madron workhouse. Climb Chûn's wide walls and investigate its defences; revel in fabulous views across the fields, a medley of greens, golden gorse and vibrant purple heather down to the sea.

But Chûn is dwarfed by massive Castle-an-Dinas (SW 945623) near St Columb Major in mid-Cornwall, a 20-acre hilltop fortress built with three huge concentric earth ramparts and ditches for defence, and a smaller fourth set; the site also contains remnants of two Bronze Age burial mounds. Castle-an-Dinas controlled the main ancient route through mid-Cornwall, as well as nearby tin-working around Roche.

Today the site is managed by Cornwall Heritage Trust and there is a small parking area for visitors.

1	Ballowall Barrow SW 355312	TR19 7NP
2	Blind Fiddler Longstone SW 425282	TR19 6AQ
3	Bodrifty Village SW 445354	TR20 8XT
4	Boscawen-ûn Circle SW 412274	TR19 6EH
5	Boskednan Circle SW 434351	TR20 8NR
6	Bosullow Trehyllys Village SW 409342	TR20 8NR
7	Bury Castle SX 135697	PL30 4DJ
8	Caer Brân Castle SW 408290	TR20 8QZ
9	Carn Brea Encl SW 685408	TR16 6SL
10	Carn Euny Village SW 403288	TR20 8RB
11	Castle An Dinas (St Columb M) SW 945623	TR9 6JB
12	Castle An Dinas (Ludgvan) SW 485350	TR20 8BE
13	Castle Dore SX 103548	PL24 2UA
14	Chûn Castle SW 405339	TR20 8NP
15	Chûn Quoit SW 402339	TR20 8NP
16	Chysauster Village SW 473350	TR20 8XA
17	Dry Tree Longstone SW 726212	TR12 6LQ
18	Duloe Circle SX 236583	PL14 4PL
19	Fernacre Circle SX 145799	PL32 9QJ
20	Gurnard's Head Fort SW 432386	TR26 3DE
21	Helman Tor Encl SX 062616	PL30 5DF
22	Hurlers Circles SX 258714	PL14 5LW
23	King Arthur's Hall SX 130776	PL30 4NR
24	Lankidden Fort SW 755166	TR12 6SH
25	Lanyon Quoit SW 430337	TR20 8NY
26	Leaze Circle SX 137773	PL30 4NN
27	Mên-An-Tol SW 426350	TR20 8NR
28	Mên Gurta Longstone SW 968683	PL27 7LG
29	Mên Scryfa Longstone SW 427353	TR20 8NR
30	Merry Maidens Circle SW 432245	TR19 6BQ
31	Minions Longstone SX 255706	PL14 5LQ
32	Mulfra Quoit SW 451353	TR20 8UX
33	Pennance Entrance Grave SW 448376	TR26 3DB
34	Pipers Longstones SW 435248	TR19 6BQ
35	Rillaton Barrow SX 260719	PL14 5LW
36	Rough Tor Encl SX 138819	PL32 9QJ
37	The Rumps Fort SW 934811	PL27 6UQ
38	Stannon Circle SX 125800	PL32 9QJ
39	Stowe's Pound Encl SX 259725	PL14 5LW
40	Treen Entrance Grave SW 438371	TR26 3DE
41	Tregeare Rounds Castle SX 033800	PL30 3LW
42	Tregeseal Circle SW 386324	TR19 7PZ
43	Tregiffian Entrance Grave SW 430244	TR19 6BQ
44	Treryn Dinas Fort SW 396223	TR19 6HJ
45	Trethevy Quoit SX 259688	PL14 5JY
46	Trevelgue Fort SW 825630	TR7 3NH

St Ives

Hay

St Just

Penzanc

Land's End

Bude

Tintagel

Launceston

Camelford

Padstow

Wadebridge

Bodmin

Liskeard

Newquay

St Austell

Looe

Fowey

Truro

edruth

Falmouth

lston

Lizard

Other hill forts are scattered across the Duchy, among them Warbstow Bury's large double-ringed example north-west of Launceston (SX 202908); Tregeare Rounds at St Kew (SX 033800); Bury Castle near Cardinham (SX 135697); and Caer Brân at Sancreed (SW 408290). Close to Ludgvan there is a second Castle-an-Dinas (SW 485350), with three defensive banks.

Near Golant on the Fowey River sits Castle Dore (SX 103548), its high Iron Age ramparts still watching over the ancient north-south trade route between Padstow and Fowey town. Of ovoid plan, the rings' widest point is around 150 yards (137m). Castle Dor's real fame though stems from much later; did its ruins once witness the legendary tragic Dark Age triangle played out between King Mark of Cornwall, his nephew Tristan and his wife Iseult?

BELOW:
CHÛN CASTLE IN PENWITH, WELL-PRESERVED AND ATMOSPHERIC; WHO MIGHT ONCE HAVE PASSED THROUGH ITS GREAT MAIN ENTRANCE?

During the same time as Cornwall's hill forts were constructed, along its coastline more defences appeared. Promontory forts were built on narrow natural headlands often bounded by steep cliffs, which Iron Age people cut off from the mainland, again using systems of ramparts and ditches. Today one of the best-preserved is at Trevelgue Head (SW 825630), just outside Newquay. With seven rampart and ditch formations it's the Duchy's most heavily-defended ancient monument, exploiting a natural chasm across a neck of land over which the old people would have used a drawbridge. Trevelgue was occupied periodically up to around 500 AD.

Gurnard's Head (SW 432386), the high outcrop near Zennor in West Penwith, bears the remains of a triple-rampart stronghold as well as flattened areas on its more sheltered eastern side, platforms once used for dwellings. Other promontory forts survive at The Rumps near St Minver (SW 934811), on St Merryn's three headlands at Winecove Point (SW 854738), and

on the Lizard at Lankidden (SW 755166), just east of beautiful Kennack Sands. Treryn Dinas fort at Treen (SW 396223) is defended by five ramparts including a huge ditch and earth bank, and is also home to Cornwall's famous Logan Rock. The promontory forts may have been used only in times of danger. Most were pretty inhospitable and many lacked fresh water supplies. For today's explorers though, in sunny weather, their beautiful coastal locations always make a great outing.

BELOW:
AT NEWQUAY, TREVELGUE HEAD PROMONTORY FORT STILL DISPLAYS ITS HUGE DEFENSIVE EMBANKMENTS. TODAY A FOOTBRIDGE CROSSES THE NATURAL CHASM SEPARATING THE OLD REFUGE FROM THE MAINLAND.

ROUND HOUSES AND COURTYARD VILLAGES

On Bodmin Moor, around the base of Rough Tor sit the thick-walled granite ruins of numerous Bronze Age round houses, together with elaborate field system remains, stone-rimmed and embanked. Easily made out, they cover a stretch of over half a mile beneath the tor's southern and western sides; more can be found to the north-west. Even for the casual walker, the sheer quantity of dwellings really is an amazing sight.

In Penwith there are several ancient villages to check out; the gaunt round house remnants of Bodrifty settlement (SW

ABOVE:
ROUGH TOR, BODMIN MOOR.

445354) are just outside Newmill. Set on gently-sloping moorland, Bodrifty's site was first occupied by Bronze Age people though today's buildings appeared during the Iron Age. A heavy-handed excavation in the 1950s unfortunately damaged the village but the spot is still good value and nearby a reconstruction has been built of a typical Bodrifty round house.

The courtyard communities of Chysauster (say it ch'ZOYster) and Carn Euny also stem from the Iron Age and are unique stone dwellings found nowhere else in mainland Britain. The houses, usually oval, consisted of several different rooms for people, animals and supplies, roofed with thatch and built with their entrances facing a gated inner courtyard. Today their walls still defy Penwith's highly-strung weather; walk on smoothed slabs into the egg-shaped spaces and you'll find evidence of hearths, conduits and wall recesses. Being wide, the walls make good platforms to see across the sites. In Cornwall there are remains of more than 20 courtyard settlements.

Chysauster hamlet (SW 473350) consists of eight courtyard houses placed in pairs with a street running between them, and a ninth house set apart. Though the chief remains are late Iron Age, there's some evidence of

earlier use. Remnants of an adjacent field system farmed by the villagers survived until the 1980s, when they were casually destroyed as modern agriculture moved in.

Carn Euny settlement (SW 403288) is preserved in a less manicured state than Chysauster, and perhaps is all the more engaging. Its four courtyard houses are intermingled with several earlier round houses. But Carn Euny is exceptional for its beautiful green-tinted fogou (from the Cornish word fogo, meaning cave), a 40-foot (12m) man-made tunnel leading to a substantial domed underground chamber; it's a truly amazing structure, though why it was built we can only ponder on. Was it perhaps a store, a refuge, or a burial chamber?

Near Chûn Castle, amid the bracken and bushes, you'll find another Iron Age settlement: Bosullow Trehyllys (SW 409342). Four courtyard houses survive,

BELOW:
THE ENTRANCE LEADING DOWN TO CORNWALL'S AMAZING IRON AGE FOGOU AT CARN EUNY.

three detached and one semi-paired with a round house, together with numerous other round houses. Bosullow Trehyllys hasn't been cleared and looms at you from the undergrowth; the village takes some finding, but the effort's well worth it.

UNIQUE STONES

Some of Cornwall's ancient sites are singular, their forms unlike any of the Duchy's other remains. Penwith's inscrutable Mên an Tol (SW 426350), the famous monument below Boskednan, probably dates from the Bronze Age. Its name means simply 'Holed Stone' and its original purpose is quite lost to us, though it may once have been part of a circle, or a burial chamber.

Old images show variations in the arrangement of Mên an Tol's stones; several times it has been meddled with. The place has long been a centre of folklore and tale, and was once said to ward off witchcraft. In times well before the NHS, to crawl through Mên an Tol's hole was thought to cure illnesses including rickets, back pain and 'scrofulous taint'; perhaps it'll make a come-back.

ABOVE:
PENWITH'S FAMOUS
MÊN AN TOL.

Just north of Gweek on the Lizard peninsula another holed stone survives, but it stands alone and on private ground. Contrasting with Mên an Tol's main feature, the tilting Bronze Age Tolvan Stone is of irregular profile while its hole is smaller at around 1½ feet across. Gweek's stone was also said to have medicinal properties.

On Bodmin Moor near the village of St Breward, King Arthur's Hall (SX 130776) is also a true one-off; no-one knows who built it or what it was for. That said, it's over 150 feet (46m) long and required considerable effort, so it must have been important to its creators. A great flattened rectangle enclosed by a banked perimeter around six feet (2m) high, the 'Hall' is bordered on its inside by numerous standing stones suggestive of chair-backs. They're not arranged in a round, and there's no table, but still the groundless myth persists of an Arthurian influence. Currently, experts believe the Hall probably dates to Neolithic times. One thing's for sure: it's a captivating place with a feeling of utter isolation, set on a wide plain against the backdrop of grand rocky hills.

BELOW:
ON BODMIN MOOR NEAR ST BREWARD SITS STRANGE KING ARTHUR'S HALL. AN EMBANKMENT ENCLOSES THE FLAT RECTANGULAR AREA, WITH STANDING STONES SET AROUND ITS BORDER.

A WORD ON CROSSES

Across Cornwall, hundreds of ancient stone crosses can be found by the wayside, near stiles, on footpaths and in fields. Many are wheel-headed but have been carved with the cross symbol, while some are quite substantial and ornate; they stem from between pre-Norman Conquest and Medieval times.

In this little book it wouldn't be possible to cover the crosses which survive today; they're just too plentiful. Equally, though of interest, for many people they don't have the pull of the bigger sites. But it's fun to spot them as you travel through the countryside, and their graceful forms continue to inspire curiosity.

ABOVE:
JUST OUTSIDE MINIONS IS LONG TOM, A LONGSTONE NEARLY 10 FEET (3M) TALL AND BEARING A DARK AGE CROSS SYMBOL, THOUGH IT MAY HAVE BEEN ERECTED DURING THE BRONZE AGE.

STONES AND GIANTS

Among Cornwall's countless legends are tales of the Duchy's ancient giants. Cornish giants were often ferocious, fighting among themselves and treating local people as vassals. But from time to time they were also passionate suitors, and a few were peaceful spirits. In Cornish folklore, giants loom large.

The giants adored big rocks and stones, using them as furniture, missiles, or to play their games of quoits. They're also said to have helped form the Cheesewring, the extraordinary granite formation at Stowe's Pound tor enclosure. Led by Uther, the local giants became enraged when a group of saints arrived in the area. The saints were popular with nearby villagers, who gladly gave them tithes previously stolen by the bullying monsters.

To settle on which group would stay, Uther and holy man Saint Tue held a rock-throwing contest, pitching in turn. The idea was to toss each great boulder atop the previous until a tower was formed. With some Divine help Saint Tue beat the giant, whose final throw fell short of the mark; Uther and his cronies duly melted into the moorland hills. But the huge rockpile is still there.

Uther wasn't the only giant who roamed the great stones. Treryn Dinas promontory fort at Treen was home to deaf-and-dumb giant Dan Dynas and his wife An' (aunt) Venna. A good couple, they offered people protection within during times of conflict. Meanwhile at Carn Brea's tor, the giant in residence, said by some to be named John of Gaunt, fought a rock-throwing feud against evil Giant Bolster of nearby St Agnes; John came off decidedly worse. Today you can still see Bolster's artillery, scattered across Carn Brea's hillsides.

LEFT:
CORNWALL'S FAMOUS CHEESWRING: LEFT,
AN ILLUSTRATION BY 18TH CENTURY
CORNISH ANTIQUARY WILLIAM BORLASE.

BELOW:
THREE CENTURIES ON:
A BRAVE VISITOR SITS BENEATH THE
TEETERING ROCK.

SOME GREAT WALKS

When you're exploring Cornwall's stones the only dilemma is where to begin; there's such a choice of location and spectacle. In Penwith, try setting off from the little parking area at Bosullow Common (SW 418344), between Madron and Morvah. Tramp east-ish for the Mên an Tol, pass the Mên Scryfa standing stone, and follow the undulating moorland track. Beyond Boskednan's circle you'll discover Bodrifty village; finally you'll arrive at Mulfra quoit, with its beautiful outlook across Penzance to St Michael's Mount.

Alternatively cross the road from Bosullow and head for the parking spot at nearby Trehyllys Farm (SW 408337). Take the footpath – indicated by a big white-painted rock – for the climb to Chûn Castle and its neighbouring quoit. Both the Chûn and Mên an Tol paths form part of the Tinners' Way, the early route to the coast for tin and copper mined around St Just.

The walk from Chapel Carn Brea's car park (SW 386281) – not to be confused with Carn Brea near Redruth – to Carn Euny begins at Penwith's westernmost hill, near St Buryan. There you'll find a big Neolithic burial site, though it's somewhat mangled after fearsome Victorian examination. On a clear day the view is fantastic; 30 miles over the water you'll see the Isles of Scilly while on the Lizard, Goonhilly satellite station's dish antennas glint in the sunlight. Leave the hill and walk eastward across low-lying Tredinney Common, sprinkled with gorse and heather; via a disused quarry and an ancient holy well, you'll arrive at the Iron Age village.

Alternatively, if you're on Penwith's south coast call on the Merry Maidens, their accompanying Pipers, and Tregiffian entrance grave. They're within walking distance of each other, while you might also take in the granite harbour and twinkly sea at nearby Lamorna Cove.

Some places are easy to find: Chysauster and Carn Euny are well-signposted while waymarks lead to other sites. Across Truthwall Common outside Trewellard, good footpaths lead to Carn Kenidjack's great fissured stones, and gently down to Tregeseal circle. Kenidjack is great for a picnic; out of the wind, nestle in a rocky sun-trap and gaze across the moor's patchwork colours.

A few miles north-east, Zennor village makes a perfect start for your tramp up the rocky hill to the quoit. Once you're back, healing liquid refreshments are available from the village's ancient pub, while at the nearby café delicious cakes are on hand. To be sure these amenities stay up to scratch, I take the trouble to test them regularly.

On Bodmin Moor a great base for the day is Minions village, with its neat shop, pub and restaurant; all are friendly with good service. Like Penwith, the Minions area has

an embarrassment of ancient riches: the Hurlers standing stones, Rillaton barrow, the climb to Stowe Pound's bizarre sculptures and the Cheeswring. From the hill there's a magical view across the village and its antiquities, as well as mining ruins and granite quarries of long ago.

Rough Tor too makes a good starting-point for investigating the stones, with its handy car-park, but take your own provisions or you'll have to go without; the nearest shops are several miles away at Camelford. Again the choice of walks and sights is amazing: circles, round house dwellings, a stretch to King Arthur's Hall, or up to the summits and enclosures. On the flatlands between the hills though, even in fine weather, it can be wet underfoot so good boots are best.

It's easy to overlook places away from the two main centres but if you're visiting the Lizard, Dry Tree standing stone is really worth a call. From the nearby car park (SW 731211) decent paths take you via the ruins of a Second World War radar station and along Goonhilly's perimeter; the great disused satellite dishes sit still and forlorn. Beyond the great longstone, the trail continues across moorland toward a wind farm. Press on to discover yet more remains: this time, believe it or not, remnants of a First World War airship base.

FOR THOSE WHO DON'T WALK TOO FAR

If you have young kids with you, or a companion who's not great at walking, sadly some of the stones are too challenging to reach. It's a double-edged sword; many of the sites have stayed reasonably intact and we have them today because they're so remote, untouched by agriculture, mining, or passers-by. But several monuments are accessible by car and can be enjoyed by everyone.

In Penwith, Tregiffian entrance grave is by the side of the minor B3315 road near Lamorna, and there's a parking area along the way from where you can spy the Merry Maidens circle. Lanyon quoit is set near two lay-bys, with only a low stile to cross.

ABOVE:
MERRY MAIDENS CIRCLE NEAR LAMORNA, UNDER A DRAMATIC CORNISH CLOUDSCAPE. THE STONES ARE EASY TO SEE FROM THE ADJOINING PARKING AREA.

But one of the best western sites for access is Ballowall Barrow, found at the end of a tiny clifftop road outside St Just signed 'Carn Gloose'. There's parking, and even thoughtfully-provided benches and tables for all to use; the surrounding scenery and seascapes are gorgeous. Take a picnic and gaze out at the Atlantic waves battering Cape Cornwall. Alternatively, as you loll in the hot sun and consider trying another crab sandwich, watch laden hardy types toiling up the picturesque cliff-face.

On Bodmin Moor, Minions' mysterious longstone is by the roadside; the Hurlers circles are just a short flat walk from the village car park, often surrounded by sheep or barrel-shaped ponies. Just off the A30 the Trippet Stones can be viewed from a handy lane, along with an inspiring outlook across the plain toward distant hills. At Looe, Duloe's gleaming white circle is accessible along a good footpath while across at Trethevy, again the great stone is conveniently near to the road.

BELOW:
TRETHEVY QUOIT HAS PARKING CLOSE BY. A FEW MILES AWAY ARE THE MAJOR PREHISTORIC MONUMENTS OF MINIONS.

THINGS TO DO NEAR THE STONES

You may like to break up your day exploring the stones and head off to discover places nearby. Around both main areas of Cornwall's ancient activity there are many different things to see and do.

A short drive from Rough Tor, call at Davidstow's amazing Cornwall at War Museum. It's built on part of the old Second World War airfield; you'll be astonished at the size and scope of the exhibits. Near the Hurlers you'll find Minions' own Heritage Centre, housed in an old mine-engine building, and between Bodmin and Lostwithiel a rather larger venue: one of the most impressive Cornish country houses, Lanhydrock.

In Bodmin itself, visit the gruesome old Gaol where more than 50 people were hanged; today it's open to the public and said to be haunted. Across the town, the Bodmin & Wenford Railway is Cornwall's only full-size railway still using steam locomotives. It's a welcoming place and the engines are beautiful reminders of times past. Opposite the station is Cornwall's Regimental Museum, which tells the story of the Duke of Cornwall's Light Infantry and holds a fine collection of medals, weapons and uniforms.

In West Penwith, near Pendeen village, Geevor was the area's last working tin mine; today it's an absorbing heritage centre with the chance to go underground into the old workings. On the south coast at Porthcurno, the Minack open-air theatre is built into the cliff edge, a unique location with gorgeous views across the sea toward the Lizard. Visit during the day just to enjoy the venue, or watch a production there but take big cushions; the seating's solid stone.

On the outskirts of Newlyn near Penzance is Trereife (say it Treave) House, a predominantly Queen Anne manor with fine gardens to enjoy. For people interested in Cornwall's mining history, both West Penwith and Bodmin Moor are scattered with wonderfully atmospheric ruins of the old workings.

ROUGH TOR'S WILD ROCK FORMATIONS
HAVE TO BE SEEN TO BE BELIEVED, WHILE
AROUND ITS BASE IS A TREASURE-TROVE OF
ANCIENT REMAINS. BUT SEVERAL DIFFERENT
ATTRACTIONS ARE ONLY A SHORT DRIVE
AWAY.

HAPPY EXPLORING!

O ver my time discovering Cornwall's ancient treasures I've met many fellow-explorers, from porridge-fuelled marchers to young families out for a muddy trudge. Encounters can be slightly surreal, but always cheery. At Zennor quoit once I was offered hot refreshments by German holiday-makers taking a breather; they'd carried every imaginable item of expedition gear up the great hill, including a teapot. A visit to the Mên an Tol didn't cure my cold, not really the stone's fault since I was too big to scrabble through it. But at least my squirms and struggles entertained some grinning Maori visitors, who took a photo which they kindly sent me as a souvenir. Hmm, thanks guys.

But often there are no people; pause to listen and the only sound is birdsong, or the wind. As well as the stones and scenery you'll find wildlife: brown mottled buzzards, forever

BELOW:
BODMIN MOOR: THE TRIPPET STONES
SIT PEACEFULLY ON THEIR PLAIN.
IT'S A GREAT AREA FOR WALKING AND
PICNICKING, WITH OTHER ANCIENT SITES
NEARBY.

patrolling with cold all-seeing stare; perhaps a lizard at rest on warm rocks; along the path a bold stoat, sitting up with front legs waggling.

There's no rush to see everything at once. Cornwall's beautiful stones have stood for thousands of years; they'll be around for a while yet. Bask in the atmosphere whether bracing or sublime, let the elements soothe or assault you. The ancient sites are a world away from busy beaches and organised entertainments, especially in high summer. On the moors there are no ice-creams or pasties, but take a packed lunch and soak up the serenity; you'll want for nothing.

TOP:
BOSKEDNAN'S SENTINELS IN WEST PENWITH. THE NEARBY TRACK TAKES YOU TO DING DONG MINE OR DOWN TOWARD THE FAMED MÊN AN TOL.

BOTTOM:
GREENBURROW PUMPING ENGINE HOUSE AT THE HISTORIC DING DONG MINE.

RECOMMENDED READING

Ian McNeil Cooke, *Journey to the Stones*, Mên an Tol Studio 1996. Describes nine different West Penwith walks, covering various ancient sites and terrains. Informative and beautifully illustrated.

Peter Stanier, *The Minions Moor*, St Ives Printing and Publishing Company 2007. Thorough survey of the wealth of walks and sights to see around the Minions area.

Craig Weatherhill, *Cornovia: Ancient Sites of Cornwall and Scilly*, Halsgrove 2009. A detailed study of all Cornish antiquities, engaging throughout, with great coverage too of the wider historical context – a winner.

Find out about ancient Cornwall's stone crosses in the five-book *Cornish Cross Series*, a regional gazette by Andrew Langdon, published by the Federation of Old Cornwall Societies.

WEBSITES FOR MORE INFORMATION

For further information on Cornwall's ancient stones, check out:
- Cornish Ancient Sites Protection Network: a charitable partnership formed to look after the Duchy's sites and monuments. www.cornishancientsites.com
- Heritage Journal: created to promote awareness and conservation of prehistoric sites in Britain, Ireland and beyond. www.heritageaction.wordpress.com
- Save Penwith Moors: a group campaigning for sympathetic future management and unobstructed open access of the western stones' moorland home. www.savepenwithmoors.com

MAPS

For those not using GPS, paper maps are essential to find your way across Cornwall's moorland, particularly Ordnance Survey Explorer Series (1:25 000, 4 cm to 1 kilometre) Sheet 102 – Land's End, and Sheet 109 – Bodmin Moor.

PLACES TO VISIT NEAR THE STONES

Bodmin Moor Area:
* Bodmin Gaol: www.bodminjail.org
* Bodmin & Wenford Railway: www.bodminandwenfordrailway.co.uk
* Cornwall's Regimental Museum, Bodmin: www.cornwalls-regimentalmuseum.org
* Davidstow Airfield and Cornwall at War Museum, Davidstow: www.cornwallatwarmuseum.co.uk
* Lanhydrock country house and estate: www.nationaltrust.org.uk/lanhydrock
* Minions Heritage Centre, and the wider Caradon Hill Area Heritage Project: www.chahp.blogspot.co.uk

Penwith Area:
* Geevor Tin Mine, Geevor: www.geevor.com
* Minack Theatre, Porthcurno: www.minack.com
* Trereife House and gardens, Newlyn: www.trereifepark.co.uk

BELOW:
THE HURLERS STONE CIRCLE, BODMIN MOOR.